KIND FRIENDS LEND AN EAR

Ashtrees

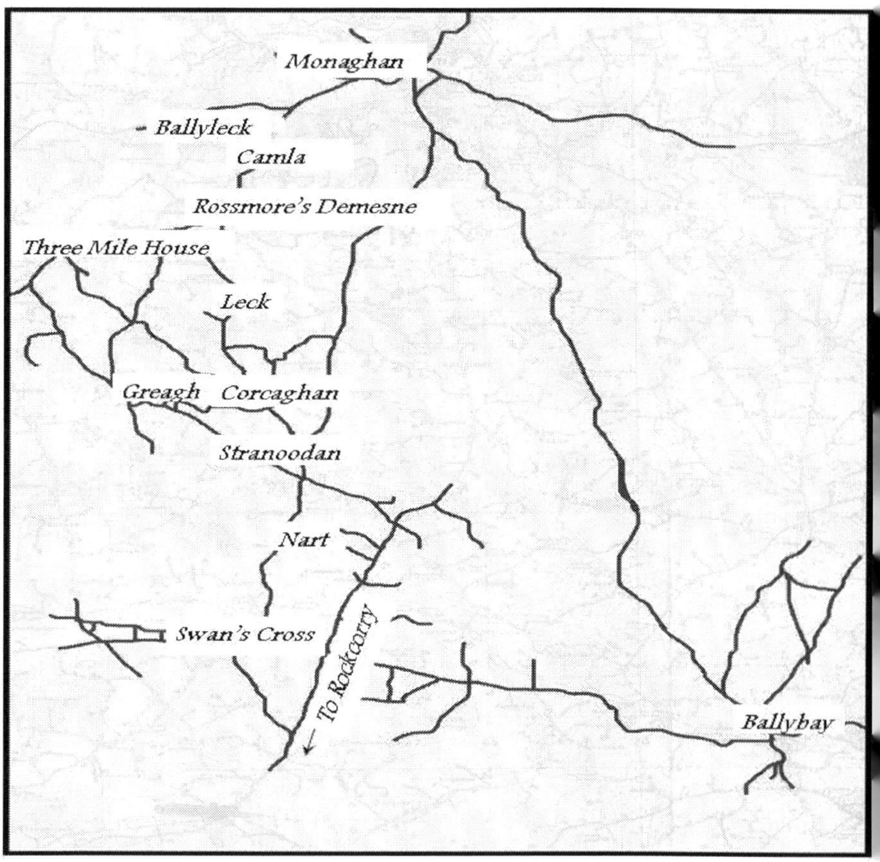
Monaghan
Ballyleck
Camla
Rossmore's Demesne
Three Mile House
Leck
Greagh
Corcaghan
Stranoodan
Nart
Swan's Cross
To Rockcorry
Ballybay

KIND FRIENDS LEND AN EAR

Songs and Stories from County Monaghan

To Bob
For old times sake!

Fergus Woods

Published by Ashtrees May 2016

ISBN -978-9575858-7-4 paperback

www.ashtreespress.com
www.monaghansongs.com

Cover design Adam Stanway
Cover photo Gerry Ruddy

Contents

Acknowledgements

First to the singers, especially Tommy McCabe, and also Kathleen Duffy and Annie Gavin, whose songs are the inspiration behind this book.
To the other members of the McCabe family, especially Michael (RIP), Dympna (RIP), Maureen and Tom for their friendship and hours of conversation over many years. Without their input this project could not have happened.
Gillian McPherson who played an equal role with me in collecting and recording the songs.
Dr.John Moulden for his suggestions and help with background information.
Una Woods and Tony Barbour who formatted the text and organised the publishing of the project.
Una Woods for her untiring revisions of the text and advice.
Gerry Ruddy for his excellent photos of the session at the McCabe home on June 2 1968
The Irish Traditional Music Archive (Dublin), especially Danny Diamond, for transferring the collection from reel to reel tape to digital format.
Donal O'Connor at Red Box Recording Studios, Belfast for his work on the song recordings including enhancement of the original performances made on reel to reel tape.
Chris Fulton for his development of www.monaghansongs.com
Mackie Rooney for sharing his knowledge on Monaghan songs.
Clones Library for providing access to the Mountain Lark columns in Northern Standard back issues.
Kevin Delaney for his assistance in this research.
Mary Durkan for her help with the later sound recordings and general encouragement.
Adam Stanway and Alice Woods for the cover design for the book.
Ken McMahon for permission to use his painting Céili at Ardara.

Claire McCabe, Maureen McCabe, Tom McCabe and Mary Durkan for singing some of the songs for the sound files.
Monaghan County Council for hosting the book launch in The Market House, Monaghan.
The Sunflower Public house for hosting the Book launch in Belfast.
The venues, especially The Sunflower Folk Club, the Fountain Bar and the Belfast Singing Circle, who have provided me with opportunities to sing these songs and keep them alive.

Preface

In the Belfast of the sixties, before the troubles distracted us, you could go to 'folk clubs' seven days a week, sometimes more than one. We were mad for singing and we were mad for songs; a new song was prized. We scoured books, learned from records, and we got the idea that, in the countryside, just beyond us, there were singers and communities that kept the songs alive.

In the hope of hearing real singers, we went to Fleadhs: County, Provincial and the All-Ireland. Singers were difficult to get to know; it needed an unusually open-minded singer and an unusually persistent and sensitive young stranger from the city. But, on the way to the Ulster Fleadh in Cootehill, in 1968 such a conjunction occurred. The singer was Tommy McCabe of Swan's Cross, Monaghan, the central figure in this book and the young stranger was Fergus Woods, its compiler and editor. During several visits many songs were given and received; then distractions; work and family.

Eventually, the songs won out, though by then all the singers had died. Fergie recovered contact with the McCabe family and, during many visits, pieced together a fuller picture of Tommy McCabe, the man, father, farmer and musician, and his community, than had been possible in the days when all that seemed to matter were the songs.

The driver of this project has been Fergus Woods but the fuel has been contributed, first by Tommy McCabe, Annie Gavin and Kathleen Duffy, and then by Tommy's family. In bringing this collection of songs and their background to the attention of you, the reader (and, hopefully, singer) we owe thanks to Fergie, to the extended McCabe Family and the people of Swan's Cross, Co Monaghan – a small place, but not inconsiderable.

John Moulden

Introduction

Courthouse Bar Monaghan Town

On the 13th of April 1968 I was travelling with a group of friends to the Ulster Fleadh Cheoil in Cootehill, Co.Cavan. We stopped off for refreshments at the Courthouse Bar in Monaghan town.

Standing at the bar beside us was a slight, elderly gentleman with a jaunty hat. He was drinking a glass of beer and clutching a parcel under his arm. While waiting for his bus home he struck up conversation in a free and easy way and when the subject of the fleadh was raised he declared his interest in the music and admitted modestly that he knew ‘some old songs’. Naturally I became immediately interested and said so. He introduced himself as Tommy McCabe and issued us with an invitation to call out to his home and see him.

Two days later I made the journey from Cootehill to Tommy’s house, not without some difficulty! Accompanying me were Gillian McPherson (member of Folk Union and later to have a successful career as a singer/musician in London and France, where she now resides), Tom Hickland (member of Winnowers Folk Group along with myself and later to join the highly successful Five Hand Reel), Teresa Sturgeon (Tom’s girlfriend) and Ray Maguire (also member of the Winnowers and now resident in the United States where he continues his involvement with traditional Irish music). Eventually we found the house at the top of a laneway which ran up from the old schoolhouse off the Cootehill-Monaghan road near Swan’s Cross.

Tommy greeted us warmly and introduced us to his daughter Dympna and married son Michael. The conversation soon came round to the music and Tommy talked nostalgically of bygone days when the entertainment was a night’s playing and singing. He lamented how many of the musicians and singers had been forced to emigrate, mostly to seek work. Others had died or simply put away their instruments as the old rural communities experienced extensive change, mainly due to social and economic factors. A small percentage did still perform at weddings, house parties and pub sessions when the opportunity arose.

Tommy admitted that he had sung on only a few occasions over recent years and it transpired that he had also played the fiddle and tin whistle. He talked of the pride a singer would have in bringing a new song into the neighbourhood.

After much interesting conversation he was prevailed upon to 'give us a verse or two'. He obliged with two songs –'Jackson and Jane' and 'Rossmore's Demesne'- which he claimed came from his repertoire of around two hundred songs!

He had a high-pitched voice and his singing used little ornamentation. An absence of teeth contributed to his singing style. His son Tom recalls how, on a visit home from England where he was working, he asked his father why he was not wearing his false teeth. 'Sure it feels like wearing an ass's shoes!' was Tommy's response.

We did not record on this occasion but Gillian and I arranged to return to Tommy's farmhouse as soon as possible.

A few weeks later we arrived, armed with a borrowed reel to reel tape recorder. Tommy greeted us enthusiastically and seemed to be pleased that we wanted to hear his songs. His preparation often included playing the particular melody on the tin whistle. Other members of the family who were present provided useful prompts for him to sing certain songs. His son Michael on fiddle and son-in-law Dessie Gavin on button accordion also contributed to a great day of song and music.

On that day and on a number of subsequent visits we collected the songs included in this book, mostly from Tommy but also some from his cousin Kathleen Duffy and his daughter's mother-in-law Annie Gavin. The songs ranged from local to more widely known, including a number of Scottish songs. Some were short, some long, some were sad, some funny. But not a verse was forgotten, nor a word missed.

The recollections I recorded from members of the McCabe family from 1996 until very recently, are a vital part of this collection. Michael, Dympna, Maureen and Tom provided me with invaluable insights into their father and his life.

Michael McCabe

Tom and Maureen McCabe

During these conversations it emerged that Tommy had written songs about local events and characters. For whatever reason he had never mentioned this to me! I include one of these which Tom was able to remember. The family is still trying to piece together others. Regrettably they were never written down.

As far as possible the words given are the ones sung by the singers. A few exceptions occur when a word or phrase cannot be made out or seems to make no sense. On these rare occasions either a word obtained from another source is inserted, or one that fits logically. Sometimes this exercise was not without its difficulties – which involved listening repeatedly to the unclear word or phrase, or searching for a version of the song in other collections.

Unfortunately the task was not undertaken while the singers were living so they could not be asked. Of course changing words either intentionally or unconsciously is part of the folk tradition. I realise I have unwittingly changed some parts of these songs when I sing them myself.

This has been a labour of love for me, something I regret not completing some years ago, before Tommy, Dympna and Michael passed on. I owe all of them a huge debt of gratitude for their hospitality, their generosity and for sharing their songs and stories. I have tried to ensure the songs do not die by including them in my own repertoire.

Gillian McPherson has recorded three of Tommy's songs on her CD *Common Ground (2002*) and Tom Hickland performed one on *Five Hand Reel's Earl of Moray LP (1978).*

It would be so rewarding if any readers would pick up these songs and sing them, like Tommy and the others did.

Tommy McCabe, from the townland of Nart in the parish of Corcaghan, was born on February 22nd 1899. He was a year old when his father, also named Tommy, died. As he grew up, having no brothers, Tommy junior had to take on most of the farm work. He married a local Nart girl, Bridget Smith and they had eight children before Bridget died in 1958 at the age of fifty two. 'Her death was hard on him', son Tom told me. 'He always did the outside work, she was the homemaker - so he had to take on that role as well.'

Tommy was a man of many talents. He was a farmer, a horseman

who was not enthusiastic about the tractor and a carpenter. He roofed and thatched houses, built byres and outhouses and could do stonework. He also worked at the cooper's, repairing threshing machines in the big byre.
For recreation he sang, played the fiddle and tin whistle and step danced. He trained Hibernian bands to play flute music.
Tommy was an avid reader and could readily quote poetry. He could read music and was proficient in the use of shorthand, perhaps useful in jotting down songs! He also acted in local productions.

Tommy McCabe as a young man

There were often parties in the McCabe household and Tommy would be invited to other houses where music and song were the norm. 'He learned many songs as a young man and they became part of him', daughter Maureen recounts. 'He would rehearse songs while ploughing the field with the horse or milking the cows. If he forgot some lines of a song he would go off to the likes of his cousin Kathleen Duffy and return with the complete song.' He had learned some of his songs from Kathleen's father Frank Murphy.

Tommy told me how he would get together with Kathleen, Frank Finlay, Johnny Maguire, Mrs Rocks and others for a function at the local hall in Corcaghan. Stephen Mc Phillips would be MC and the festivities would go on late into the night. Tea, bread and jam would be available, with light from hurricane lamps. Singers, musicians and step dancers were called upon to perform. The next evening the scene could be recreated in Three Mile House or Rockcorry with their own local performers present. Another opportunity for the local singers and musicians was provided when travelling shows arrived in the area. Often they were used to entertain the audience before the show got underway.

Tommy gathered up songs at these events as well as at Hibernian band rehearsals he attended in Co. Armagh. He often came home pleased that he had a new song. Maureen remembered that he had a wee pencil with which he would write down the beginning of a verse on the back of his hand. But largely the learning was done by remembering a song through hearing it a few times. Tommy told me he could know a song after hearing it twice!

In later years when the old venues for singing and music-making were a thing of the past, Tommy did participate in some pub sessions in McKenna's in Monaghan town in the company of fiddlers Peter Farelly and John McKearney and accordion player Johnny Murphy. The renowned fiddler Tommy Peoples sometimes attended.

Tommy also occasionally attended a monthly session at Rice's in Ballybay where regulars included Sarah Makem, Mick Gaffney (fiddle) and his daughter Lily (piano).

Tommy had an accident on his farm and died in hospital from complications on Christmas Day 1971.

THE SONGS

Céili at Ardara

Reproduced from a painting by Padraic Woods RUA

SONG TITLES

In the notes preceding each song I have often quoted the Roud Index number for the particular song or a variant of it. This refers to a Folk Song and Broadside Index compiled by Steve Roud which is included on the *Vaughan Williams Memorial Library* website. A search of the Roud number will bring up all versions found of the song. However whether one song is a version of another is not always entirely clear. The song names in this collection are those used by the singers, although they are sometimes called by different names elsewhere.

I have also referenced other sources related to the songs but I do not claim to have provided a comprehensive account of all known references.

Punctuation in the song texts has been reduced to a minimum. It is only used where I felt it would aid interpretation. How the words were delivered by the singer can be heard in the recordings of the first verses (see below). But each singer is free to choose how the song is delivered. Moreover the same singer can vary interpretation (as well as actual words) of the same song from performance to performance. I have an example of that with two recordings of Tommy McCabe singing 'The Lass among the Heather'.

The Recordings

I have not provided musical notation for the songs as is customary but a recording of the first verse of each song can be found on **www.monaghansongs.com**

Where available and quality is acceptable original recordings have been used to give a flavour of how these singers sounded. Other singers, including myself, have provided the tunes for the rest of the songs.

The songs were recorded over a three month period in 1968 on a four track reel to reel recorder, except for 'Bill Beattie' which was recorded from Tommy's son Tom in 1995 and 'Is this Corcaghan at all?' sung by Kathleen Duffy, which the McCabe's found recently on a reel to reel tape. Some of the recordings went missing shortly afterwards but fortunately I had already transcribed the words of the songs from the lost tapes and learned the tunes, except for 'Pat Molloy' and 'Lovely Jimmy'. The airs for these were supplied by family members after Tommy's death.

To the best of my knowledge the only other people to record Tommy singing were Robin Morton and Frank Harte. I introduced them to Tommy in a Clones pub during the All Ireland Fleadh in June 1968. They recorded four songs on this occasion and I have used Robin's recordings of 'The Flower of Virginia' and 'The Bloomin' Maid of Rockcorry Town' in the sound section on the website.

The tapes were converted to digital format in 2013 by the Irish Traditional Music Archive in Dublin. For the purposes of the current project Donal O'Connor at Redbox Studios Belfast digitally enhanced the first verse of each of the songs. These are the recordings I have used to provide the tunes for the songs in the book.

Tommy's Favourite Ballad

1 Matt Hyland

There was a lord lived in this town
Who had a fair and comely daughter
She fell in love with a young man
Who was a servant to her father
And when her father came to hear
He swore he'd make him leave this island
And the young girl thought her heart would break
If she should part with young Matt Hyland

The lord discoursed with his lady fair
One night within their bedroom chamber
Young Hyland I will send afar
I fear our child she stands in danger
The lady gay in ambush lay
With grief oppressed she lay repining
She says my father I'll deceive
For to protect my young Matt Hyland

And straight she went to his bedside
Demanding him for to awaken
Arise young Matt and go away
I fear this night you will be taken
For I just heard my father say
In spite of fate he will transport you
So arise and go before it's day
You know my love I do adore you

Must I now leave my servitude
How can I go without my wages
Must I leave my dear he cried
And roam a poor and forlorn stranger
Here's fifty guineas in bright gold
Sure that is what my father owes you
So take it Matt and go away
I wish to God I'd gone before you

Young Hyland he the purse received
He says my dear it's sad to leave you
Some noble lord may captivate
The lass I love so fond and dearly
He threw his arms around her waist
And round his neck her arms were twining

No neither lord nor duke I'll wed
When you are gone from me Matt Hyland

In deep embrace till near the dawn
The couple sat long time discoursin'
As if to ease their troubled hearts
The tears like rain down their cheeks were coursing
She says dear Matt it's sad to see
You go away so broken hearted
But perhaps some day we'll meet again
They kissed, shook hands and then they parted

' Twas thus those lovers severed were
That he might elude transportation
Now that he was gone perhaps for e'er
Her sad heart knew no consolation
As time went by she then betook
To roam the woods alone and silent
As in her dreams she cried aloud
Bring back, bring back my love Matt Hyland

The lord discoursed with his daughter then
I did not know how much you loved him
I give you leave to bring him back
Since there is none you'll style above him
She wrote a letter in good speed
To him her heart it was inclining
So off to church this couple went
She made a lord of young Matt Hyland

Tommy's father, also called Tommy, was a singer. Tommy being only one year old when he died would not have remembered hearing him sing. But his mother passed on some of his father's songs to Tommy (she did not sing in public herself) and told him stories about the singing sessions.
As a tenant of Lord Rossmore his father was invited to an annual function held in the Canal Stores which was a thank you to the tenants for supplying grain in lieu of rent. On these occasions he often sang a duet with James 'Duckman' Cairns - their party piece being 'Matt Hyland'. In fact his father was so well known for singing this song that he acquired the nickname 'Matt Hyland' in the locality.
As a result Tommy himself sang 'Matt Hyland' and told me it was a very special song for him. He often sang it as a duet with Stephen Mc Phillips.

The Roud Index has ten references for the song (*Roud 2880*). I have not come across a version with as many verses as Tommy's.

Humorous Songs

2 The Draperstown Fleas

Now kind friends lend an ear to the truth I declare
And attention pray pay to the same I'll relate
In the month of July I from Dublin did drive
And from there made my way to Draperstown straight
At the end of my route I was tired no doubt
And went off to my bed to sleep at my ease
But to my sad mistake I was kept wide awake
By those bloodthirsty murdersome Draperstown fleas

I had scarcely laid down when the thousands came round
On my back and my body my legs and my side
All night they were knawin' and brutally chawin'
Until the whole neighbours was forced to make rise
The blankets were fallin' the pillows were crawlin'
They were so alive they were near in a blaze
The curtains were shiverin' the sheets they were quiverin'
O what did I see but these Draperstown fleas

We got so affrighted a candle was lighted
And a message was sent to the landlord in haste
To rise and to quell them if not to expel them
If not his poor bones we would warmly baste

The landlord in a hurry he sent for Mick Murray
Said Mickey Mavourneen get up if you please
And you Tommy Fletcher to help us to butcher up
Some of these bloodthirsty Draperstown fleas

Well Mick from his wallet he pulled out a mallet
I pulled up the blankets unto the hearth stone
He starts like a thresher or else a stone smasher
Until that he left these boys some broken bones
And Tom with a pounder as flat as a flounder
He laid into these tyrants that sore me did tease
Likewise Mrs Fletcher as smart as a switcher
She walloped away at these Draperstown Fleas

Well for two hours or better these boys we did batter
We cut them before us like moss on a stone
Right madly they fought us and sometimes they caught us
And one time I thought we would have to run
But with gallant adherence and good perseverance
We battled till daylight and ne'er stood to gaze
Then we fled from the action in horrored distraction
And cursed the sad night of the Draperstown Fleas

Now I must abridge and I'll leave you to judge
O didn't I suffer from this hairy tribe
I paid for my lodgin' and off I went dodgin'
The mock of the village the talk and the jibe
Till I go to my grave neither landlord or knave
Will e'er me enslave till death ends my days
But my bed I'll inspect and my hide I'll protect
And I'll think of that night with the Draperstown fleas

Tommy was particularly fond of humorous songs. 'The Draperstown Fleas' has been found in various versions where the place name changes e.g. Palmerston, Kilkenny.
I have not come across the 'Draperstown Fleas' elsewhere.

3 Pat Molloy

Now Pat Molloy an Irish boy up from the County Clare
He thought he'd go to London just to see the wonders there
Sure they tell me that London is a very pretty place
Bedad sez Pat I'll go and see if that might be the case
Now Pat shook hands with all his friends and kissed his colleen dear
He left the sod begob he did and he never shed a tear
Sez Paddy I will know the road if ever I am sent
To that mighty place in London called the House of Parliament
With me fol di diddle dil di diddle fol di diddle day
Fol di diddle dil di diddle fol di diddle day

When Paddy reached that city he was taken by surprise
The beauty of that city fairly lit up Paddy's eyes
As he was walking down a street and round a corner he went
He met a nice young cockney with a donkey selling delph
This young undaunted cockney he would not let Paddy pass
Sayin' speak unto your brother and he pointed to the ass
Bedad says Pat I didn't think I had a brother here
And then he stooped and whispered into the donkey's ear
With me fol etc

Now when Pat was speakin' to the ass me boys what did he do
He dropped an oul chew in its lug he did me boys that's true
The ass went mad upset the cart broke all the earthenware
The young undaunted cockney went crazy clean and fair
He called for a policeman to take poor Pat in charge
Sayin' an Irish vagabond like that should never be at large
Bedad says Pat I'm charged with far more than I did
I was speaking to my brother just doin' what I was bid
With me fol etc

Come come says the magistrate have none of your nonsense here
Come tell us what you whispered into the donkey's ear
Bedad says Pat your honour that question I won't refuse
I've always heard that asses they are very fond of news
Well I told him that in Ireland we had our wrongs redressed
And by the cruel tyrant we were no longer pressed
We had got rid of landlords and Ireland to ourselves we had
And when the donkey heard the news I'm damned but he went mad
With me fol etc

The magistrates in shame were forced to hang their heads
When they listened to the answer that Irish Pat had made
I see said the chairman that a noted rogue you are
But for your clever answer I'll dismiss you from the bar
With me fol etc

This song deals with the use of the Irish Language in signage on carts and the ensuing conflict with the law. It is a theme which appears in other songs, including 'Oldcastle Fair' which my father sang.

4 Nothing to do with me

Well perhaps now of what I sing about I hope you will not frown
For I don't like this nasty wee way of running people down
My motto is to do what's right no matter what I see
Let people do as they've a mind to do
It's got nothing to do with me

Chorus
For I never interfere no matter what I see
Let people do as they've a mind to do
It's nothing to do with me

There's Mrs Brown lives down the town keeps lodgers four or five
For to do a decent wee job this woman does contrive
Some of the lodgers grumble of no sugar in their tea
Whether there is or not my boys
It's got nothing to do with me

Chorus

The other night as I strolled out along the Monaghan road
I saw lad and lassie by the hedge as they stood
They were a loving couple by the moonlight I could see
But what they were doing or talking about
It's got nothing to do with me

Chorus

I once knew a wee lassie about the age of twenty four
She married an old gentleman he is eighty six and more
Well now they've got a baby and the old man's filled with glee
But whether it belongs to him or not
It's got nothing to do with me

A simple little song which Tommy enjoyed singing, especially the risqué nature of the last verse as he saw it.
There is a broadsheet version in the *Bodleian Library (Roud 5315)* which, from the names of people featured in the song, is set in England.

5 The Green Garters

In the city of Belfast lived a smart guy called Arthur
Just listen a while till you hear what comes after
He courted six fair maids friends and acquaintances
Determined to show them the way of repentance
Chorus
Ry tur a ny a tur a ny addity
Fol di riddle addity tur a nye ay

Now each one of the six that young Arthur had chosen
Sure he played a trick on the even half dozen
He bought them green garters to please them completely
In under their borders he bowed them so neatly
Chorus

O he took them away o away to an alehouse
And brought them in one by one just as he was able
He first rang the bell and then out came a waiter
He ordered some drink to be brought to the table
Chorus

He took over a chair set it down in the middle
He says my wee lassies I'll read you a riddle
Then liftin' his glass up he drank to bold Arthur
Likewise the wee lassie that wore the green garters
Chorus

O indeed says Miss Jane then it's me he admires
O no says Miss Kate I will call you a liar
Then lifting their clothes up all in due order
Sure each of them wore them right under their border
Chorus

Well one took his hat and another his favour
Another his coat and called him a deceiver
The next took his shirt and another his breeches
Till he yelled in despair you're a bundle of witches
Chorus

He was left all alone in the alehouse lamentin'
He was left all alone in the alehouse for the reckonin'
When in came the landlord and he says cousin Arthur
Don't sport any more with those funny green garters
Chorus

I recorded Tommy singing this song on a beautiful summer's day, sitting on a chair in the yard outside his house. I had brought a group of musicians along from the All Ireland Fleadh in Clones in June 1968, including Tommy Gunn (fiddle), Seamus Tansey (flute), John Carlos (flute), Sean Quinn (piano accordion) and Tom Hickland (fiddle). There followed a great session of music and song lasting into the evening.

I have not come across this version of the 'Green Garters' anywhere else. There is a broadsheet version of the song *(Roud 6667),* which includes the lines:
'He courted six maids and he called them all cousins
He got five with child out of the half dozen.'

Tommy's version does not go quite so far!

The session outside Tommy's house.

Fergus Woods (standing foreground), Dympna McCabe (standing against wall), Tommy Gunn (seated foreground, fiddle), Sean Quinn (seated behind Tommy, accordion), John Carlos (standing, flute), Seamus Tansey (seated, flute).

Tommy McCabe (standing at the doorway), Gillian McPherson (standing in the middle), Tom Hickland (seated foreground, fiddle).

Boy Meets Girl

6 Blackwater Town

As I went out walkin' one evening in June
The birds sang so sweetly and the fields were in bloom
I spied a fair damsel as Phoebus rode out
As she stood on the road close to Blackwatertown

I stood as the night fell this fair maid did sing
And the woods and green valleys in echoes did ring
The thrushes and blackbirds their sweet notes did sound
To welcome this fair maid of Blackwatertown

Said I pretty fair maid if with me you'd agree
We'd both join in wedlock and married we'd be
I'd dress you in satin and your joys I would crown
If you would consent to leave Blackwatertown

O to marry to marry you know I'm too young
And besides all young men have a false slandering tongue
My old aged parents on me they would frown
If I would consent to leave Blackwatertown

Wi' your lovely brown eyes and dark curlin' hair
My heart you have wounded and caught in a snare
And if you don't wed me I would roam up and down
And my heart it would linger round Blackwatertown

I've described this fair damsel but won't tell her name
I have told you her dwelling and you might find the same
My talent is feeble so my pen I'll lay down
And I'll style her the primrose of Blackwater town

A very common theme in folksong involves a young man strolling out and encountering a beautiful young female who captivates him with her charms.
Tommy sang a number of songs of this genre including 'Blackwater Town', which he had also heard sung as 'Sweet Keady Town'. This seems to be an offshoot of 'The Banks of Callan near Sweet Keady Town' as sung by Sarah Makem.

7 Rollin' in the Clover

Now I'm what you call a swell and I am without a care
I left my native city just to seek a change of air
To a pleasant countryside I then did stray away
Where I met my charmin' bride all among the hay

Chorus
All among the hay lads all among the hay
All among the hay in clover
Courtin' in the green fields with a pretty girl
There's nothing like a roll among the clover

O where nature's beauty blooms it's sure to be admired
I went out one evening I was feeling rather tired
As graceful as a fawn she did stand in my way
With a cask of barleycorn all among the hay
Chorus

Said I my pretty maid would you come along with me
We'd go off together and married we would be
If you give me your consent you'll live to bless the day
That we met by chance alone all among the hay
Chorus

O no young man says she you're a stranger unto me
Unto a simple country girl you shouldn't make so free
If I give you my consent what would my father say
Better move or we'll be found all among the hay
Chorus

Still I pestered she gave in and soon her heart I'd won
There's not a man who cannot win a woman with his tongue
Soon the bells will chime out for our wedding day
Then I'll sow my wild seeds all among the hay
Chorus

It seems that the young man has not successfully wooed the 'primrose of Blackwater Town'. There is a different outcome in 'Rollin' in the Clover' which is a more lighthearted approach to his courtship of the girl.
In fact the conclusion is given away by the end of the first verse where the writer states:
'Where I met my charmin' bride all among the hay.'

There is a broadsheet version of this song in the *Frank Kidson Manuscript Collection (Roud 18372).* An added ingredient in that version is the arrival of a rival as the couple roll in the hay, who has to be thrashed to fend him off!

8 The Lass among the Heather

As I was comin' home from a fair in Ballymony-o
I met a comely lass she was fairer than Diana-o
I asked her where she lived as we jogged along together-o
Upon the mountainside she replied among the heather-o

O lassie I'm in love with you, you have so many charms-o
O lassie I'm in love with you your bosom to me warms-o
The bonny blink of your blue eye your person is so clever-o
I'd fondly wed with you O my lass among the heather-o

Now do not think young man said she that I'd be easy spoken to
And do not think young man-o that I'd be easy taken-o
I'm happy and I'm well with my father and my mother-o
To take a bonny lad for to wed me from the heather-o

O lassie condescend to me and do not be so cruel-o
O lassie condescend to me give a kiss to me my jewel-o
If I would give you one you would surely ask another-o
Just take it if you want replied the lass among the heather-o

Well mark you what came next-o the youth he was so clever-o

He didn't quit the lass till he'd ta'en her from the heather-o

And now this pair's got wed they live in peace and pleasure-o

Young Bessie minds the day she met her lad among the heather

In 'The Lass among the Heather' there is also a satisfactory ending where:
'This pair's got wed and they live in peace and pleasure-o.'
The version closest to the one Tommy sings is Jeanie Robertson's 'The Fair O Balnafannon'.
John Moulden states that the original version was penned by the Glenavy (Co Antrim) schoolteacher Hugh Mc Williams and he includes it in his booklet, *Songs of Hugh McWilliams, Schoolmaster, 1831 [p15].* Here the fair was in Ballymena whereas Tommy had Ballymoney.
Robin Morton included Tommy's version in his publication *Folksongs Sung in Ulster [p7].*

9 The Flower of Virginia

As I roved out one evening down by a purling stream
For to view the meadows charming, each one none rarer seen
I spied as fair a damsel as e'er my eyes did see
As I drew near a village clear called lovely Virginia

Her eyes they were transparent so lovely to behold
Her yellow hair in ringlets fell, like waves in links of gold
Her carriage neat, her limbs complete, her aspect mild and free
Like Venus clear she did appear the flower of Virginia

Said I my pretty fair one your beauty does outshine
Fair Helen or Diana, I wish that you were mine
If you'll agree my dear said he and come along with me
We'll make no delay but this very day leave lovely Virginia

But this fair one she made answer and this to me did say
You might be acting pleasant, my virtue to betray
'Tis not my small share of beauty should *e'er entrancing be*
And although you smiled you have my heart beguiled the flower of Virginia

No no my pretty fair maid I will never be untrue
To beguile a maid and be afraid, I'll not begin with you
Here is my hand my dearest maid and come along with me
We'll make no vow but I'll wed you now my flower of Virginia

The italicized words in the second last verse represent my attempt to make sense of a phrase I cannot make out from Tommy's singing.

Virginia (pronounced Virginny) Co. Cavan is the setting for this song. It eulogises a beautiful young lady as seen through the eyes of her suitor. At the time of writing I have not come across another version of this song or anyone else singing this version. As with many similar songs, including a number in this collection, the author shows a knowledge of classical references to (for example) Helen, Diana, Venus.
Eamonn Murray, chairman of Comhaltas Ceoltóirí Éireann, published a series of articles under the pen name 'The Mountain Lark' in the *Northern Standard Newspaper* (1933-1942). In many of these he included a song and extensive commentary.
He includes a song 'The Blooming Maid of Collegeland' (March 8th 1935), where a similar extensive use of classical images is employed.
The second verse is:
'If Jason had once seen this maid
The Golden Fleece he'd ne'er pursue
Leander swim the Hellespont
Nor lovelier creature for to view.'

This was a common feature of 19th century love songs in the tradition and would suggest that the writers had some knowledge of Greek and Roman mythology and that the rural people would have understood them.

10 The Bloomin' Maid of Rockcorry Town

One fine morning ranging for recreation
Through Lord Corry's handsome demesne
I heard a youth make his lamentation
Which showed his bosom was set on fame
His tender heart had been captivated
And Cupid seemed on his grief to frown
For in his song he oft repeated
The bloomin' Maid of Rockcorry Town

All you imps and swains of the Irish nation
Pray pay attention one and all
Onto these same lines which I'm goin to mention
In praise of a maid that did me enthral
Her name to mention I do decline it
Less snarlin' critics should unto me frown
But her habitation you'll easily find it
For she resides near Rockcorry Town

It bein' on a fine and bright summer's morning
As Sol broke forth from his crimson shade
When his golden beams the hilltops adornin'
There first I spied this blooming maid

The early lark was aloft ascending
And other small birds sang sweet all round
With their soft notes blending curlews calls were rending
To greet the maid of Rockcorry Town

I would describe this fair gem of nature
Was I adequate with my feeble pen
There's no dissension in this fair creature
Like other maidens who ensnare young men
For her modest blushes would pierce Cupid's armour
Her smiles his darts which she throws all around
Since by those charms I was captivated
Can I blame the maid of Rockcorry Town

No costly robes clad this fair young virgin
No diamond rings on those hands did wear
No Spanish shoes or silken hosiery
But on the silvery dew her neat feat were bare
But poverty can ne'er eclipse the beauty
With which fond nature so freely crowned
Pardon me my ladies but it is my duty
To extol the maid of Rockcorry Town

O were I a king or a mighty emperor
With a gallant army at my command
Or were I possessor of all the treasure
That e'er was gained by sea or land
Or was I owner of the gold of Ophir
Without reluctance I'd lay it down
And I'd freely ramble this wide world over
With the Bloomin' Maid of Rockcorry Town

This is also an ode to the stunning beauty of a young maiden encountered by a young man on his morning ramble. In my hunt for a printed version of the song, not least to attempt to decipher a couple of words where Tommy's singing is unclear, I came across a broadsheet version held in the *Bodleian Library, Oxford*. The very three words I was looking for were blurred so I was no further forward, a mystery in itself! John Moulden then tracked down a broadsheet version in the *Alexander Turnbull Library, Wellington, New Zealand*, and the words were clarified - 'grief to frown'.
I subsequently discovered a version of the song in '*Monaghan Songs of Yesteryear*' *[p73]* compiled by Mackie Rooney. It is not stated from whom the song was collected.

11 Rossmore's Demesne

O as I went out walking one evening in May
Around Rossmore Castle I chanced for to stray
I spied a fair damsel and neatly stepped she
Down the banks of a river by the weeping ash tree

Said I pretty fair maid are you queen of love
Or are you Diana that fell from above?
Come tell me plainly from whence you have came
To wound a true lover on Rossmore's demesne

She answered me kindly I'm not queen of love
Nor am I Diana that fell from above
I'm a shepherd's one daughter and from Camla I came
And I came just to walk around these beautiful plains

Said I pretty fair one my time is so free
It's for to go with you your flocks for to see
Down to yon meadow where we would not be seen
We could pluck the sweet nuts off the hazel so green

O no she made answer you can't come with me
Down to yon meadow my flocks for to see

As for pullin' the sweet nuts I would think it a shame
We might both be transported from Rossmore's demesne

O my queen I would crown you with jewels so rare
With timely persuasion the garland to wear
I won't wear your garland and would wish to explain
That my love is a stranger on Rossmore's demesne

At the foot of yon high hills his castle does stand
It is well decorated from the top to the sand
With cut stone and marble and diamonds so bright
It would pilot a sailor on a dark winter's night

Farewell pretty lass since my love you deny
From these green woods and valleys I'll bid you goodbye
My ship lies in Belfast ready to sail
She'll bear me back home with a free pleasant gale

Farewell to you Camla a place I respect
Likewise to Tyholland and old Ballyleck
No more o'er these green fields my horn I will sound
I will now bid adieu to the cry of the hound

The young man is wandering round Rossmore Castle (near Monaghan town). He meets the 'fair damsel' but his wooing is rejected. Apparently he lives abroad, as
'My ship lies in Belfast ready to sail
She'll bear me back home with a free pleasant gale'.

In the last verse he bids farewell to Camla where he used to hunt. This is a little confusing but suggests that he has returned for a visit and would have stayed had the girl accepted his advances.
I also collected a version of this song from Annie Gavin. In her version there is no mention of the young man heading off to Belfast to board a ship.
Tommy claimed the song was composed 'by a man called Owens from an adjoining townland'.

Leaving the Land

12 Edward Boyle

All you tender hearted Christians of high and low degree
Likewise all wounded lovers come sympathise with me
Well here I am bewailing the lad I do adore
Who has now fled from my arms bound for Columbia's shores

In the county of Fermanagh in the parish of Roslea
In the townland of Greaghawarren near the mountain of Sliabh Beagh
He was reared by honest parents who for him sore did toil
Alas they're sunk in sorrow for their son, loved Edward Boyle

Well do I mind in summertime in the pleasant month of May
When Flora's flowery mantle did deck each meadow gay
When everything looked charming all nature seemed to smile
Then I parted with my own true love my charming Edward Boyle

O long will I remember the day he went away
His friends likewise his neighbours they all did him convey
Into the town of Monaghan when he left the Shamrock Shore
All peace be with you Edward Boyle will I ever see you more

This country has got lonely now since Edward went away
For he was the pride of Collegeland and the flute so well could play
His comrades all both great and small all swear they'll leave this isle
In hopes once more on Columbia's shore to meet with Edward Boyle

My curse attend Columbus who first found out the shore
And to that ship called Mary Coe that sailed in days of yore
From that time down there's many are found in sorrow, grief and toil
To lament and mourn their true love's return like me for Edward Boyle

Now to conclude and finish all you fair maids that's true
'Tis never place your mind on gold as sometimes lovers do
For was I possessed of a pot of gold that's in St Patrick's Well
I would part it all with pleasure for one glimpse of Edward Boyle

Often the reason for emigrating is not overtly stated but the songs normally record the sorrow and pain of the emigrant and/or those left behind.
This song is placed in Co Fermanagh and tells of the grief felt by the true love of Edward Boyle who is sailing to America. This is a popular ballad sung by several singers in Ireland.

A version is published in *The Mountain Lark column (February 25th 1935)* and in it Eamonn Murray claims he met a man who as a boy was acquainted with the same Edward Boyle. He remembered him as a celebrated flute player. 'As good a man as ever carried a creel to the bog or a sack to the pit. But the hunter's horn or the twirl of the flute interested him more.'
But after a few bad harvests, with many others, he was trudging in despair to the emigrant ship.

Tommy told how someone emigrating, usually to America, would be an occasion for a get-together where neighbours would assemble in a local house with singers, musicians and a barrel of porter in attendance. It was like a wake and could last for a week. A grand aunt of Tommy who left in the 1850's took three months to travel across the Atlantic. Her name was Mary Mc Bride and her portrait hangs in Tommy's home.
Usually the emigrants never returned. An exception was Paddy McCabe, a first cousin of Tommy, reared a field away. He went off to America and married a rich lady. Every few years he returned home and threw big parties. Everything in the locality was put on hold. There was a free bar - tapped beer and a hogshead of whiskey. The women dreaded it as their men folk would be away drinking and making music for days. Paddy would go into Monaghan and buy a side of sheep for cooking.
Tommy told a story about Paddy coming back from shooting and spotting a row of ducks coming up from the river. The ducks belonged to Tommy's mother but 'he lifted his gun and shot them all!' She ran out of the house horrified but was consoled when he put his hand in his pocket and gave her three times the value of them. He took the ducks home and cooked them for one of his parties.
Paddy is buried in Corcaghan in a lead coffin and was embalmed under a glass cover. According to Tommy the coffin was reopened twenty five years later and he was in his dress suit with a gold pocket watch, looking as well as he did when he was alive!

13 Lovely Jimmy

The high hills of Derry are lonely today
Since my lovely Jimmy has gone far away
He's gone out to Australia his fortune to gain
May heaven protect him till he comes back again

The first place we met was in a shaded wood
Where the thyme and the wild flowers grew around where we stood
With his big coat wrapped round me shaded from the wind
Tell me now Lovely Jimmy what has all changed your mind

The next place we met was not far from my home
In my own father's garden in the county Tyrone
With the flowers all bloomin' on that evening so fine
Tell me now lovely Jimmy what has all changed your mind

Annie my dear Annie sure our courtship's in vain
For I never intend for to meet with you again
For it's not my intention of taking a wife
So farewell dearest lass we must both part for life

Jimmy, lovely Jimmy do you mind the day
When you came to my window and stole my heart away
You told me that you loved me above all female kind
Tell me now lovely Jimmy what has all changed your mind

Annie my dear Annie I never did intend
In my own native country my lifetime to spend
I must seek fame and fortune in some far distant clime
So that's now the reason why I've changed my mind

A bunch of blue violets I'll gather with care
And a garland of flowers I will wear in my hair
And if ever I meet him I'll crown him with joy
And I'll kiss the sweet lips of my dear Irish boy

This song also goes under the name 'The High Hills of Derry', 'The High Walls of Derry' or 'Johnny, Lovely Johnny' and has been recorded by Cara Dillon and Vincent Doherty among others.

In this case Jimmy is going off to Australia 'his fortune to gain'. Sadly for his jilted lover Jimmy declares that their relationship is at an end and he does not intend to return to her. But as indicated in the last verse she will not lose hope of them meeting again.

14 Sweet Little Maid from the Town of Kinsale

'Twas at Queenstown our ship with its engines in motion
It bantered away like a threshing machine
And before us the Lee and a broad stretch of ocean
Behind us the high hills of Kerry so green

Weepin' and wailin' took up every minute
And that evening dies out with a sorrowful wail
Except for a colleen that sang like a linnet
That sweet little maid from the town of Kinsale

She was bright as the dew on a fine summer's morning
A fair type of colleen from out of this vale
Free and light hearted all warning cares scornin'
That sweet little maid from the town of Kinsale

She could dance jigs and reels with the grace of a fairy
Her little feet twisting like hooks and like eyes
O how her laughing blue eyes bein' so airy
She lifted up many a breast full of sighs

The cabin was filled with the cream of the peerage
Great duchesses and lords of the best I'll go bail
O what did the wee girl the queen of the steerage
The sweet little maid from the town of Kinsale

O the question was how could she be so light hearted
While others lay pinin' and moaning about
Or had she forgotten the loved one she parted
Faith when we landed we quickly found out

There was a handsome gossoon full of joy there to greet her
O how are you Terry I knew you'd not fail
How my mouth watered the way that he faced her
The sweet little maid from the town of Kinsale

There is a different twist here compared to most of the leaving songs. The 'sweet little maid' is showing no grief for 'the loved one she parted'. We discover that there is a 'handsome gossoon' waiting to greet her on the other side. We know that the maid is from Kinsale and is leaving from Queenstown Harbour (Cork), but we do not hear of her destination.

I have discovered a printed version of the song published in the *Washington Times (July 10th 1913),* under the title 'The Maid from Kinsale', credited to a Eugene Geary.
Recently I have come across a recording of this song on YouTube under the title 'The Maid of Kensale'(sic). The singer is *Shaun O'Nolan* and from the label displayed on the video the recording

was on *Columbia Records* and made in 1923. O'Nolan was a vaudeville performer, a piper and singer, originally from Wicklow who spent a lot of time in America. Further information on O'Nolan can be found on a thread on the Mudcat website, www.mudcat.org.

15 My Sweetheart in the Old Country

By Killarney's fighting waters where love sighs it flows merrily
There dwells one of Erin's daughters, who is waiting to hear from me
Yesterday I got a letter full of funny words you can see
Begging me to not forget her, her own sweetheart in the Old Country

Chorus
Blow ye winds ye white sails bending
Bear my message across the sea
'Tis a message I am sending
My sweetheart in the Old Country

Many tender words were spoken as we parted on the quay
When I asked her for a token, take my poor broken heart said she
And if you can find one better just return mine back to me
But be sure address your letter, your sweetheart in the Old Country
Chorus

O of pleasures I had many and of sorrows I had my share
But the thoughts of my wee lassie, cheers and comforts me

everywhere

I will go and find a casket for the jewel so dear to me

And I know for whom I'll ask it, my sweetheart in the Old

Country

Chorus

In some ways this song has a music hall quality about it, even the title.
I have only found one reference to the song and it is intriguing!
In an edition of the *Buffalo Courier February 10th 1896* there is an article about Jack Quirk who is awaiting trial on two murder charges. To pass the time he likes to sing.

"He has a heavy baritone voice, which though uncultivated is melodious. In his captivity his heart seems to have flown to the land of Erin, where his childhood was spent. One of the prettiest Irish ballads he sings is called My Sweetheart in the Old Country. The refrain runs,

'Then blow ye winds the white sails bending
Bear this message across the sea
It's a message I am sending
My sweetheart in the old country'."

So clearly the same song. I do not know what fate befell Jack!

16 The Dang Boat

Well here I am an Irishman just landed here today
I thought I'd see yez all for a while so I came across the sea
They tell me Scotland is the place where everything is free
Bedad says I, if that's the case that's just the place for me

So away I went a rovin' bent
I paid my fare near Jefferson square
I then took a floater a beautiful boat
My father was there he was tearin' his hair
My mother was cryin' my sweetheart was dyin'
My mother in haste threw her arms round my waist
Sayin' paddy a stor kiss your mother once more
Before you go away across that big sea
You're sure to be drowned you'll never be found
You'll make a fine dish for some beautiful fish
The haddock and hake will dine on your face
Och paddy a stor what caused you to roam
On that dang boat that first brought you over

Well I kissed sweet Judy Connor then I jumped on board the boat
Steam went up, sails were set and soon we were afloat
The pipes they struck up gaily they lost their darlin' boy
My mother she cried bitterly and indeed boys so did I

Well first came thunder then came rain
I wished myself at home again
The sea it was growlin' the ship she was rollin'
At every blow to the devil she'd go
At every minute she was slap at the gibbet
You can guess my emotion all alone on that ocean
The ship goin' to bale me no-one for to save me
There in despair I was sayin' a prayer
When a wave from behind as quick as the wind
Struck me on the neck put me down on the deck
When the captain passed by ara master says I
Take me home to my mother my sister and brother
Says I stop the ship I'll get out and I'll walk
So they brought me some pork on the end of a fork
Says Paddy eat that no says I it's too fat
I lay down on the floor and a big oath I swore
If ever I get home no more I would roam
On that dang boat that first took me over

This is a more lighthearted approach to sailing away from Ireland. The anxiety is present even though the young man is only going to Scotland! But the song does reflect the issue of moving across the water in search of work. I have seen a version of it where the destination is England rather than Scotland. John Moulden, in his booklet *Thousands are Sailing*, under the title 'The boat that took me over' *[p24]* has the young man heading to America.
Robin Morton includes Tommy McCabe's version in his book *Folksongs Sung in Ulster [p48].*

Going to War

17 Famed Waterloo

It bein' on a May morning as day was a dawning
By a clear purling stream as I chanced for to stray
It was there I espied a most beautiful damsel
And I lay down and down boys to hear what she did say

The song that she sang it would make the valleys ring
And the small birds around her their sweet notes did subdue
Sayin' the peace it is proclaimed and the war it is all over
Yet young Willie's not returned from famed Waterloo

If William Smith's the name of your hero of fame
Then beside him I rambled all through the long campaign
Through Portugal and France we fought on together
He was my chief comrade from marching in Spain

When that in Belgium the French forces landed
Two Irish soldiers stood radiant and true
We fought for three long days until at last he was defeated
That great, great Napoleon of famed Waterloo

On the fourteenth of May sure the battle had ended
And thousands lay dying on every battle plain
The bullets flew like rain and the cannon loudly rattled
It was by a French soldier your true love was slain

I saw him on the plain he lay bleeding and dying
And scarce had he time to bid me adieu
And these were the last words that ever he repeated
Farewell lovely Molly wherever you may be

And when that she heard of this sad conversation
Her two rosy cheeks grew as pale as a swan
And when that he saw her in such a sad condition
He flew into her arms sayin' I am the man

For here is the ring that between us was broken
In the middle of all dangers it reminded me of you
And when that she saw it she flew into his arms
Sayin' you're welcome home dear Willie from famed Waterloo

A specific reason for leaving home, going off to war is a common theme in folk song.
This can be categorised as both a Napoleonic song and a 'broken token' song.
Under the title 'Plains of Waterloo' it has been recorded by

several performers including Shirley Collins and Martin Carthy. The same story is told in the song 'Her Mantle of Green'.
The young men returning from war were apparently quite expert in disguising their appearances, as well as their voices, to conceal their true identity from their forlorn lover!
It should be noted that the Battle of Waterloo took place on the 18th June 1815, not the 14th May as the singer has it.

18 The Bonny Bunch of Roses

As I roved out one evening it being in the merry month of June
When all the feathered warblers their notes did sweetly tune
I espied a pretty female she was seemingly in grief and woe
Consulting with young Bonaparte concerning the bonny bunch of roses- o

O one so young Napoleon and he takes his mother by the hand
Pray mother stay with patience until I am able to command
I will raise a terrible army through tremendous danger I will go
And in spite of all the universe I'll conquer the bonny bunch of roses-o

O look son don't speak so venturesome for England is the heart of oak
O England, Ireland, Scotland their unity will ne'er be broke
O son think on your father's fame in St Helena his bones lie low
And son you follow after so beware of the bonny bunch of roses o

But his aim for power it was so great his greed to conquer he could not subdue
All nations *mothers they fold and quail*, his fame resounds the whole world through

So he raised a terrible army and o'er the frozen Alps did go
He says I'll conquer Moscow and return for the bonny bunch of roses- o

He had kings and knights to guard him and likewise generals so stout and strong
He was so well provided that he could sweep the world along
O but when he came to Moscow it was overpowered by a fall of snow
And Moscow town bein' in a freeze 'twas there he lost the bonny bunch of roses- o

So adieu adieu sweet mother now that I'm on my dyin' bed
Had I lived I would have prospered but I must now drop my youthful head
But while my bones do moulder and weeping willows o'er me grow
The deeds of young Napoleon will ne'er stain the bonny bunch of roses-o

This is one of the best known and most popular of the Napoleonic songs. It has been recorded by many singers including Seamus Ennis, A.L.Lloyd, Sam Larner and Fred Jordan. One theory is that the title refers to the British Isles.
Tommy's lyrics include some differences from other standard versions *(Roud 664)*. This has caused a problem with a few words

where I am unsure what Tommy is singing. The line in question does not appear in any of the other versions I have come across. The relevant words are italicized.

Tommy was very fond of this song and played me the tune, which he described as ‘a difficult enough old air’, on the tin whistle before he was encouraged to sing it.

According to *The New Penguin Book of English Folk Songs*, a broadsheet version reveals George Brown as the author of this song, which was set to a melody derived from an Irish love song ‘An Beinnsin Luachra’ (The Bundle of Rushes).

19 When the Roses bloom Again

Roamin' in the gloamin' when the roses come in bloom
There was a soldier and his sweetheart staunch and true
Her heart was filled with sorrow, for her thoughts were on tomorrow
Then she pinned a rose upon his coat of blue

Do not ask me love to linger for you know I cannot stay
Don't you hear the sound of bugle call me away
And sweetheart don't be sighin', if I'm not among the dyin'
I'll be with you when the roses bloom again

When the roses bloom again beside the river
The mockingbird he sings again each refrain
In the days of old lang syne, I'll be with you sweetheart mine
I'll be with you when the roses bloom again

From the rattle of the battle came a whisper soft and low
From a soldier who had fallen in the fray
I'm dyin' chaps I'm dyin' and you know I'll have to go
But I want you to promise before I pass away

There's a far off distant river where the roses come in bloom

There's a maiden will be waiting there in vain

And there I'll have you take me so be faithful don't forsake me

For I was to be there when the roses bloom again

Here the soldier does not survive the war to return to his fair maiden 'when the roses bloom again', as he promised.
The song is clearly American in some of the language used, and in fact a version has been recorded by Johnny Cash among others. It is interesting that it found its way into the repertoire of Tommy McCabe.

Scottish Songs

20 Glasgow Nell

In Glasgow Green there lives a lass called Nell, called Nell
She works in Robinson's Mill ye ken, hersel' hersel'
She's as bonny a lass as ever you seen
Or e'r tripped over Glasgow Green
And she's aye sittin' knittin' at the door

Chorus
For she won my heart while she was sittin' and knittin'
The time that I was smokin' and spittin'
And ever since then the time has been flittin'
For Nellie she lives next door

The first time I put marriage to my Nell my Nell
She told me to go and ask her mother mysel' mysel'
For sure says she there's none too nice
For I got into a row about twice for she said I was gettin' too great
With the laddie that's livin' next door
Chorus

Well now I have got married to my Nell my Nell

We've got a wee house in Glasgow Green by oursel' by oursel'

And for little children we have three

And the youngest of them sits on my knee

We're both sittin' chattin' at the door

Chorus

Tommy had never been to Scotland but local people he met at the musical evenings brought back songs from their time working there, often in Glasgow, and Tommy had learned them.
As mentioned, Tommy was fond of the light humorous song and this fits into that category. I have not seen or heard this song elsewhere.

21 Bonnet of Blue

In fair London's city where fortunes are made
There's a famous Scots regiment goes out on parade
There's one lad among them I wish that I knew
For my heart is away with his bonnet of blue

And early this morning e're I left my bed
I called in young Sal she was my waiting maid
I said dress me as neat as your two hands can do
Till I go seek the lad in his bonnet of blue

My love he marched by with a gun in his hand
I tried to speak to him but he would not stand
I tried to speak to him but from me he flew
My bonny Sots lad in his bonnet of blue

'Tis out of the army I'll buy your discharge
And out of the army I'll set you at large
O if you prove constant and to me prove true
My bonny Scots lad in your bonnet of blue

If out of the army you buy my discharge
If out of the army you'd set me at large
O if I prove constant and if I prove true
O what would my own little Scots lassie do

For I have a lass in my own counterie
I never will slight her for her poverty
For if she prove constant to her I'll prove true
I'd ne'er bring a stain on my bonnet of blue

I'll send for an artist from London to come
I'll have my love's image taken down in full bloom
And in my own chamber I'll place in full view
My bonny Scots lad in his bonnet of blue

This song connects to Scotland in so far as the young soldier who is the object of the author's admiration is a member of a Scottish regiment based in London. He rejects the young girl's advances saying that he has a 'Scots lassie' in his 'own country'.
It is a little different in that it is usually the young man who is the disappointed lover.
There are versions of this song to be found in the *Bodleian Library Broadside Collection (Roud 819).* The location is the North of England as opposed to London. The soldier is not named in this version but 'Charles Thompson' or 'Charles Stuart' is a name given on broadsheets.

22 The Blantyre Explosion

On Clyde's bonny banks as I lately did wander
Round the village of Blantyre I chanced for to roam
I met a fair maid she was dressed in deep mourning
And sadly lamenting the loss of her love

I stepped up to her said I my fair jewel
Tell me the cause of your misery and woe
I fear you're lamenting the loss of some loved one
The name and what happened I'd like for to know

With sighin' and sobbin' she then made me answer
John Murphy kind sir was my true lover's name
Twenty one years of age and of nice good behaviour
He went up to Blantyre to work in the mines

On the eleventh of September the day I remember
He left in health and strength to his work he did go
But on that fatal morning without one moment's warning
Two hundred and ten in cold clay did lie low

There was fathers and mothers widows and orphans
In Stonefield High Blantyre with cause for to mourn

Old aged parents for their sons they loved dearly
By a great explosion they never returned

Springtime brings forth all the flowers of the summer
The leaves in their beauty so lovely and fair
Primroses and snowdrops are gathered together
On my true lover's grave I will transplant them there

With my tears I will water these fine lentil flowers
And earnestly pray to the ruler on high
For here in this wide world my days they are numbered
And soon by his side in cold clay I will lie

Now the day was appointed and friends were invited
O had he lived he'd have made me his bride
But by a great explosion that occurred in High Blantyre
No more will we meet on the banks of the Clyde

This is a fairly widely known ballad of a mining disaster which occurred in the village of Blantyre near Glasgow on the 22nd of October 1877. Over 230 miners died when a shaft collapsed.
Tommy's version has 11th September as the date, while John Maguire's version in Robin Morton's *'Folksongs Sung in Ulster'[p9]* has 11thDecember.
Another demonstration of how folk song is not always reliable history!

The ballad is found in print form (without music) as '*The Sorrowful Lamentation of Jane Sneddon for the loss of her lover, John Murray, at the late disaster at High Blantyre*' and is credited to a John Wilson.

Sporting Heroes

23 Jackson and Jane

You Monaghan sportsmen attention draw near
To a few simple verses you quickly shall hear
It's the deeds of a hero I've heard people say
And they call him Hugh Jackson from Creeve in Ballybay

His mill kilns and barns they do cut a fine show
His cloth to the north and the city does go
For folding and bleaching he exceeds them all
And his cloth is first sent to the great Linenhall

Now more of his praises I'm goin' to explain
If you listen awhile I'll sing about Jane
You may search all through Ireland from Derry to Clare
But you'll ne'er find an equal for Jackson's grey mare

He went into the stable to saddle up Jane
Arise my wee lassie you must go again
For twice you have won it and may do it still
And roll it in splendour on the plains of Cootehill

'Twas on Bellamount racecourse we next see this mare
All ready for action as swift as a hare

Proud Jackson that ragman that e'er called at Creeve
He feared for his bets on that day I believe

The jockeys were mounted and all in a row
If you had to be there when off they did go
The bets they were making ten guineas to four
That the cup back to Creeve wouldn't come any more

When Jane she heard this sure her mettle did rise
O'er the hedges and ditches like lighting she flies
And with a loud neigher these words seemed to say
You Bellamount sportsmen I'll show you the way

As Jane and her jockey sped on round the course
Sure Jane and her jockey they seemed to discourse
Says Jane to her jockey kind sir let me know
Where are my opposers or are they in view

He turned in his saddle and cast an eye round
I see by Squire Corry that Adams is down
While Dorman's black charger his jockey has threw
And the rest of your opposers they are not in view

When Jane she heard this she jogged in at her ease
To the scale where the balance and saddle were weighed
The vales they resounded for Jackson and Jane
with honours the cup comes to Creeve back again

And now to conclude and to finish my song
Here's a health to Hugh Jackson and may he live long
He's a credit to his country for the deeds he has done
And his parents are honoured with their own blessed son

Songs about sporting achievements are common in Irish folklore – usually commemorating a victory by a local hero, man or beast. Often similar events are recounted from different parts of the country.
This was one of the first songs Tommy sang for us and he preceded it with the following story of how Jane was acquired and turned out to be a legendary steeplechaser.
The fishman was delivering fish from Dundalk to Jackson's mill in Ballybay. The horse and cart were parked outside when a pack of hounds came past and spooked the horse. She broke free from her harness and, jumping the hedge, charged over the fields in pursuit of the hunt. Hugh Jackson witnessed the event, and was so impressed with the potential of the mare as a steeplechaser that he bought her from the fishman.

My research led me to the *Journal Clogher Record (1962 and 1989).* The full name of the horse was Crazy Jane and she won the Bellamount (Cootehill) steeplechase four years in a row (1804-1807).

Since the song includes the words,
'For twice you have won it and may do it still',
it would seem to place the composition of the song in 1806, before the third victory.
Important information comes from correspondence between Arthur Montgomery, Aughnamullen and Hugh Jackson Morgan, Birmingham, Alabama. The latter was a descendant of Hugh Jackson of Creeve (1783-1833), the renowned steeplechase jockey and owner of Crazy Jane.
The letter, which is quoted in the publication *At the Ford of the Birches,* states that Hugh Jackson died on a ship bound for the USA.
Hugh Jackson Morgan also revealed that he had in his possession the silver cup presented by Charles Coote and won by Hugh Jackson on six occasions.
Controversy surrounds the burial place of Jane, allegedly interred with her saddle and silver bridle.

There are two interesting footnotes.
Firstly the line:
'Proud Jackson the ragman that e'er called at Creeve', is unclear in its meaning.
P.B. O Mordha, (Clogher Record, 1962) has:
'There was never a nag, man, e'er born in Creeve
To take the cup from her this day I believe.'
A curious coincidence is that Jackson won the same race in 1809, riding a horse called Ragman.
Secondly, Tommy did not sing the last verse above, but Gillian McPherson had noted it and imagines that Tommy must have recited it to her afterwards.

24 The Leck Hare

December the fourth was the date of the year
That evening was sunny, and frosty and clear
The hounds of Corcaghan to Leck did repair
To indulge in the pastime of hunting the hare

Frank Finlay our leader, the hunt did begin
He beat every rush, bush, whitehorn and whin
The beagles gave voice as they scented the air
And sweet was the sound on the calm evening air

Says Primrose to Precept, "we'll give her a thrill
And make a lap record going over Leck Hill"
Down by Ballagh and Togan the Leck hare did fly
And behind her the beagles raced on in full cry

Tullyvarney was reached and the hare in full view
And through Tullygillen like a thunderbolt flew
A fig for your howling 'tis little I care
Your efforts are futile to kill the Leck hare

I've been hunted and harried day after day
And though cornered full often I've still stole away
My place of concealment is down in Leck Lane
And in spite of your efforts I'll trick you again

At the old fort of Cavan she burst into view
And the dogs at her heels came thundering too
In solid formation they swept o'er the hill
Each straining and striving to be at the kill

Through Annaglough headland she flew like a bird
With a speed that made dogs one and all look absurd
The broad road she reached and in one bound she crossed
And the dogs are dismayed for the scent they have lost

With their nostrils dilated they rush to and fro
While the hare halts a moment to gaze at the foe
Half in pity, half in scorn, she surveys the pack
To see some rush forward and others rush back

But Primrose gives voice as the scent he has found
To the choruses commingled the hills all resound
The hare dashes forward and crosses o'er Greagh
And the pack in communion incessantly bay

Then oh, what a view boys, and oh, what a race
And oh, what a hare that is making the pace
And speak of forked lightening it couldn't compare
With the dash and the speed of the gallant Leck hare

To the cross of Drumsheeny she raced and she ran
While the crowds on the hillside all cheered to a man
Though the dogs in extreme have ceased to give tongue
True to blood and to breeding they gallop along

Now darkness is falling, the sun sinks to rest
And the glow of his parting rays brighten the west
The hare now exhausted yet leading the pack
In a moment of folly speeds back on her track

Oh now she's encircled and time's ebbing fast
On hillside and heather she's looking her last
One last look at Calliagh, one look at Slieveroe
Where in life's vim and vigour she dashed to and fro

Farewell to the fields where she oft romped and roved
To the dark sheltered valleys and the hill that she loved
Farewell to all pleasure, farewell to all care
And farewell, oh farewell, to the gallant Leck hare

The circle contracts as they dash to the kill
And their howling re-echoes from hill unto hill
And smaller and smaller the circle still grows
While the hare stands transfixed in the midst of her foes

The crowds watch in silence the end of the race
And grim consternation is seen on each face
A final step forward, the crowds give a gasp
And the Leck hare, the matchless, is captured at last

But no! like a rocket that springs into space
The panther's precision, acumen and grace
As lithe as a leopard that leaps on its prey
She soars o'er the circle and gallops away

Hurrah for the sportsmen who dash o'er the hills
Hurrah for the hunting its joys and its thrills
Hurrah for the noble who do and who dare
And hurrah, oh hurrah, for the gallant Leck hare

There are a number of similar songs for example 'The Granemore Hare', 'The Creggan White Hare','The Aghabog Hunt'.
Another local song is quoted in the *Mountain Lark column (Northern Standard, April 5th 1935):*
'On a fine hunting morning at the break of the day
Monaghan sportsmen all dressed in array

There was Rossmore and Woodwright just ready to go
And blue faced wee Bawn his merits we know.'

An interesting story is that the original Leck Hare was reworked by Frank Finlay, local fiddler and great friend of Tommy, and Tommy himself. Finlay even inserted his own name into the lyric as master of the hunt.
The original version can be found in *Monaghan Songs of Yesteryear [p24]* compiled by Mackie Rooney.
This is the reworked version as Tommy sang it.

Tommy's Composition

25 Bill Beattie

Bill Beattie is a bachelor who badly needs a wife
For months he searched around to find a partner in his life
He heard about a batch of dames from the age of fifty down
Who were ready for inspection in a home in 'Blaney town

With great determination he contacted Peter's Pat
Dressed up in his Sunday suit put on his new grey hat
He drove them fast to 'Blaney and the home they quickly found
And he interviewed the matron and she goin' on her round

And when she heard their errand a smile spread o'er her face
Two marryin' men would soon relieve congestion in the place
She rang a bell and very soon twelve damsels came in view
For close inspection by the boys but none of them would do

Now Willie he was critical and hard to please was Pat
Some were thin and ugly and others far too fat
One well-built blondie model caught Willie's eye but then
She had never ever fed a pig or even tried a hen

When asked what part he came from Willie said Cromague
And from Fox's cooking he'd got sick from hunger and fatigue
But he'd farmed a hundred acres had a stock of twenty cows
And for fear of bacon runnin' short he hogged eleven sows

Paddy waited patiently while Willie blew his horn
And said that he had tractors and mowed both hay and corn
He was drawin' milk this fifty years and that through thick and thin
If there ever came a vacancy he'd be minister for skin

The matron then said kindly you both must persevere
Patience is a virtue come back in the new year
For you look and seem to be two hard oul workin' boys
I'll keep for you a pair to share your sorrows and your joys

Now to conclude and end this rhyme as the light is growin' thick
Good luck to all the bachelor boys as they go to take their pick
May they soon be married and their cookin' troubles end
Is the dearest wish of everyone and a prayer for my dear friend

Bill Beattie was a neighbour and the story was that he was on the lookout for a serving boy to replace the one who had left, unable to put up with Bill's demanding nature any longer. For the purposes of the song Tommy changed the story to one where Bill and another neighbour 'Peter's Pat' were looking for female companions to share their lives with.
Apparently Bill was not at all pleased with Tommy's caricature!

Kathleen Duffy (nee Murphy)

Kathleen who hailed from Greagh, was a cousin of Tommy and a regular participant at the local singing sessions.
I recorded the following three songs from her singing.

26 Tammany Hall

You jolly boys of Monaghan are invited to a ball
On the 4th day of December to be held in Tammany Hall
'Twill bring unto your memory some meetings of renown
Such as one in Ballyocean and a few in Monaghan town

'Tis there you'll meet the boys from home with their colleens bright and fair
With any county in the isle I'm sure they can compare
With their witty ways and funny jokes there's none that can surpass
The boys you meet from Monaghan when they chance to take a glass

They'll talk of towns and mountains, of the huntsman and his dogs
Of craggy lands and whinny hills around through Aghabog
The blueberry rocks near Aughnacloy or a fair in Ballybay
Of rich lands near to Clones or the heather on Sliabh Beagh

So jokingly they tell their tales their thoughts for to enfold
You'd think it was Dean Swift himself or Carleton of old

But the music and the dancing it will be the best of all
'Twill far surpass all other fetes e're held in Tammany Hall

So now be sure you do attend or a splendid time you'll miss
With the boys from Castleblaney, Corcaghan and Newbliss
Inniskeen and Ballinode and Scotstown will not fail
To meet the boys from Carrickroe and some from Emyvale

The newlyweds will lead the march a splendid sight you'll see
There'll be Murphy and Maguire and also Phil Magee
And I myself I will be there I always make a rule
To meet the ones I used to know around Corcaghan school

This song recalls the nostalgia felt by emigrants from Monaghan who assembled for a gathering at Tammany Hall in New York. Tammany Hall was the name of a political organization which wielded considerable influence in the Democratic Party. Its power grew considerably with the influx of a large number of Irish immigrants to New York City. As a result the Irish began to become a significant force in American politics.

I have not heard this song sung elsewhere. Mackie Rooney has published it in his collection [p44]. He obtained it from Tommy's son Tom who tells me that he believes that his father was a co-author of it.

27 Michael Davitt

One night as I went on my rambles, from Swinford to sweet Ballinalee
I met a young maid on my travels and her name it was Mary Magee
She sighed for the rights of her country, Michael Davitt's my true Irish boy
But he's now in the prison of Portland from the lovely green banks of the Moy

As I stepped up to this fair maid, as she did walk all alone
I asked her the cause of her misery and why did she leave her old home
This fair maid she quickly made answer, Michael Davitt's my true Irish boy
But he's now in the prison of Portland from the lovely green banks of the Moy

I did know that hero Mike Davitt, he came from the parish of Straide
In the year eighteen hundred sixty seven your love was a green coated blade

I would commend that hero Mike Davitt, his country would never deny
But he's now in the prison of Portland from the lovely green banks of the Moy

So now to conclude and to finish, I hope that the day will soon come
When the landlords and cruel bad bailiffs from the land of St Patrick must run
We'll unfold our green and gold banner, and wave it o'er Erin's green isle
With respects to the brave Michael Davitt and the lovely green banks of the Moy

Michael Davitt, from the parish of Straide, County Mayo, joined the Fenian movement while a young man living in England and rapidly rose through the ranks. He returned to Ireland after a period of imprisonment and was a leader in the emerging Land League which was established to fight for the rights of the tenant farmers. He travelled widely and in the late 1870's he went to the USA where he met his future wife, Mary Yore.

They returned to Ireland in 1887 and lived in the Land League Cottage given to them as a wedding present by the people of Ireland.

Davitt died in Dublin in 1906 at the age of 60. After a large funeral his coffin was brought to Foxford, Co Mayo for burial.

One of his four terms spent in prison was in Portland, as referred to in the song. There seems to be no factual basis to a relationship with a 'Mary Magee' as quoted in the song.

Cathal McConnell in his extensive collection *I Have Travelled This Country [p103]* has included a version with an extra verse. He attributes his source as Marie McEntee (Three Mile House), an acquaintance of Tommy McCabe and a singer Tommy greatly admired.

28 The Bonny Hawthorn

It was a summer's evening and all nature seemed gay
I espied lovely Jamie attending his hay
He says my bonnie treasure will you come to where I dwell
Beside the bonny hawthorn that blooms in the vale

For it grows in the valley and it blooms in the vale
Beside the bonny hawthorn that blooms in the vale

And its hark my daily treasure to the birds in yonder grove
How contentedly they're singing and inviting each to love
Where the briars are decked with roses and perfume the fanning gale
Beside the bonny hawthorn that blooms in the vale

So come all ye lads and lassies and my Jamie loves me well
Beside the bonny hawthorn that blooms in the vale

This is clearly a variant of a song *(Roud 9268)* under the same title. The *Yorkshire Garland Group website* states that the song was popular in the Esk Valley, probably brought in from Scotland. It has been printed by a number of Scottish broadside printers.

29 Bunclody

O were I at the moss house where the birds do increase
At the foot of Mount Leinster in some silent place
By the streams of Bunclody where all pleasures do meet
And all I would ask is one kiss from you sweet

By the streams of Bunclody where they flow down so free
By the streams of Bunclody I am longing to be
A-drinking strong liquor at the height of good cheer
Here's a health to Bunclody and the lass I love dear

The cuckoo is a pretty bird it sings as it flies
It brings us good tidings and tells us no lies
It sucks the young bird's eggs to make its voice clear
And the more it sings cuckoo the summer is near

If I was a clerk and could write a good hand
I'd write to my true love and make her understand
That I am a young fellow who is wounded in love
Once I lived in Bunclody but now must remove

'Tis why my love slights me as you may understand
She has a freehold and I have no land
She has a great store of riches and a large sum of gold
And everything of beauty a house to uphold

So farewell dear father my mother adieu
My sister and brother farewell to you
I am bound for America my fortune to try
When I think on Bunclody I am ready to die

This is a widely known and performed song in Ireland. Anecdotally it was the song Luke Kelly said he would like to be remembered for.

It is included in *Anthology of Irish Verse ed Padraic Colum (1922).*

Under the title 'The Maid of Bunclody and the Lad She Loves Dear', it appears in Colm O' Lochlainn's collection, *Irish Street Ballads [No 76].*

That version is virtually identical to the one I collected from Kathleen Duffy, but has an extra verse.

Strong similarities have been noted with 'Pretty Saro', a song found widely in America.

Annie Gavin

Annie, the mother of Dessie who was married to Maureen, came from the Greenan's Cross area.
Unfortunately I only got a few songs from her reputedly large repertoire.

The following anecdote tells something of how songs were acquired.
On the one hand they were passed across and down orally, but singers could also be very protective of their songs and be reluctant to share them.
A local singer, James (The Rabbit) Greenan, sang 'Lough Sheelin Side' one evening with an extra verse Annie had not heard. She asked him for it but he refused to give it. But she heard him sing it again soon after and now she had it. Later at her daughter's wedding Annie sang 'Lough Sheelin Side' complete with the new verse. Greenan was present and in Annie's words 'he wasn't a bit pleased and stamped the floor with rage!'

30 The Gypsy Laddie

There was two gypsies in the East they sang so blithe and bonny
They sang so sweet so very very sweet they charmed the heart of a lady-o

Charlie rode home late that night inquiring for his lady
She's gone she's gone cried the old serving man she's away with the gypsy laddie

Saddle for me my milk white steed the brown one's not as speedy
That I might ride the length of the night and find out the gypsy laddie

He rode north and he rode south he rode east and westward - o
Till he overtook his own wedded wife following' the gypsy laddie

Are you goin' to forsake your house and land are you goin' to forsake your children-o
Are you goin' to forsake your own wedded lord and follow a gypsy laddie

What care I for my house and land what care I for my children-o
And what care I for my own wedded lord only followin' a gypsy laddie

Once I had a fine feather bed my wedded lord beside me-o
But now I lie in an ashy pit my gypsy lad beside me-o

She tore off the garment she wore wrapped it in a headdress-o
Sayin' I'll eat the grass and I'll drink the dew and I'll follow the gypsy laddie

A common ballad found widely in Ireland, Scotland, England and North America under various names e.g. 'Seven Yellow Gypsies', 'Raggle Taggle Gypsies' *(Roudl).*These versions all have seven gypsies.
The Child Collection contains twelve versions of the song.
Though some claim it is based on a true story – the House of Cassilis is quoted in some versions- there is no historical evidence for this assertion.

31 The Old Oak Tree

The night bein' dark and stormy and thickly fell the rain
Young Lizzie left her mother's home and came not back again
She left her mother's fireside not fearing rain or cold
The maid bein' young and fair to see but love had made her old

For three long weary weeks went by and Lizzie was not home
Which made her parents weep and think where to their child had roamed
For three long weary weeks went by and Lizzie was not found
Squire John McGowan came to hunt and bringing all his hounds

Up hill down dale McGowan rode in gallant company
Until at length they lost the fox beneath an old oak tree
The hounds began to sniff and smell and tearing up the clay
And all that whip and horn could do would not drive the hounds away

Then the gentlemen all gathered round they cried for pick and spade
They dug the ground and there they found the missing murdered maid

Her body that was pure and white was covered with wounds and blows
And from those wounds fresh blood ran down and trickled through her clothes

A knife engraved stuck into her breast all to his grief and shame
And there upon the shaft it bore Squire Mc Gowan's name
I done the deed Mc Gowan cried my soul is bound for hell
O hide her cold corpse from me and the truth to you I'll tell

'Tis true I loved young Lizzie well and by my cunning art
I won her to these vicious views and broke her mother's heart
The knife I took my dinner with I plunged into her breast
And with this stick I knocked her down I need not tell the rest

Then he turned and took one last look upon the corpse so pale
He drew a revolver from his belt and fired it in his brain
We buried him where his body fell no Christian grave had he
No priest was found to bless the ground beneath the old oak tree

A pretty grim murder ballad which has been found in broadsheet form around 1867*(Roud 569).*The Roud versions were collected in Canada and the United States as well as Ireland. There is no evidence that the event actually happened and the names of the main protagonists vary from version to version.

Mrs Gavin told me there was an old belief that a murder victim would bleed afresh in the presence of the murderer, hence:
'and from those wounds fresh blood ran down and trickled through her clothes.'
Around the same time as I was collecting this from Annie Gavin, Robin Morton had a version from a Mrs Conner which he included in his anthology- *Folksongs Sung in Ulster [p24]*. She recited the words and Robin used a tune provided by John Maguire.
This type of murder ballad is not that common in the Irish tradition but Eamon Murray in his *Mountain Lark column (May 22nd 1936)* publishes a similarly themed song 'Ellen McGuire'. The climax is recounted in the following verses:

'But the Devil's temptation
Soon entered my head
I thought to violate her
And leave her for dead;
I took out my knife
And cut off her long hair
And tied up the hands
Of young Ellen McGuire.

When I finished the murder
I returned home I own
In the shade of the woodland
I left her alone;
The birds all assembled
With a noise in the air
To lament on the loss
Of young Ellen McGuire.'

Beyond the Songs

Tommy on his land at Nart

While the songs form the central part of this book, it has been fascinating to learn about Tommy McCabe the man and the people who surrounded him, from the conversations with him and members of his family.
As mentioned earlier Tommy was many things besides a singer.

The Fiddle

Tommy was taught the fiddle by Mickey Connolly of Three Mile House who was also a singer from whom he learned songs. (Mickey's daughter was *Marie McEntee*, who was a source for *Cathal McConnell's* collection, *I Have Travelled This Country).* Tommy also learned tunes from Michael Coleman and James Morrison recordings played on the wind-up gramophone - the Talking Machine as he called it.
Tommy said that when you carried your fiddle to a session it stayed in tune but when you strapped it to your bike it went out of tune!
One of his closest friends Frank Finlay (author of the version of the Leck Hare published above) was a great fiddle player. His brother Paddy played piccolo with the legendary Michael Coleman in America. One of Coleman's reels is called 'Paddy Finlay's Fancy'.
Paddy Finlay brought one of Coleman's fiddles back from America and asked Tommy if he could repair it. But the fiddle remains in a state of disrepair in the McCabe household to this day. The date 1814 is stamped on it.
Son Tom remembers the house 'full of fiddles and bits of fiddles'. One day a salesman of farm products called to the house. He commented on the fiddles on view and it turned out he was from Sligo and played the fiddle. A brief call turned into a four hour session of tunes and chat about the music!

Another fiddle player in Tommy's circle was Robbie Haire who lived in a Church of Ireland minister's house in Three Mile House. He played in Malachy Sweeney's Ceili Band along with fiddle maestros Sean McGuire (formerly Maguire) and Brendan McGlinchy.
Maureen gave me a moving account of visiting Robbie in the County Hospital shortly before he died.

'The tears were running down my face. He had suffered a stroke and his bowing arm was completely limp. His son had brought tapes of music to stimulate him. I lifted his poor hand and kissed it. I thought of the lovely music that hand had played and the people he had entertained. He had a light bowing action and a lovely touch with his twirling wrist. Even though he was a farmer he had the fingers of a typist. He had great technique, playing in the fifth and seventh positions which was unusual for a traditional player. He had learned a lot of tunes from Pat McGuiness and Owen Connolly. Tommy had a different style of playing but Robbie admired it.'

Fiddle playing remained in the McCabe family. Michael played and we recorded some tunes from him. Another son Seamus and a daughter Nan also carried on the tradition. And the bow has passed to grand-daughter Claire, Tom's daughter.

As a young girl she played at the graveside at Sean McGuire's funeral. She now plays a fiddle given to her by the great man himself. Claire is also an accomplished harpist and singer.

Claire McCabe

Tommy the Composer

While chatting to members of Tommy's family after his death I discovered, to my surprise, that Tommy had written songs about local characters (see Bill Beattie above) and events. He had never mentioned this to me, whether through humility or because he thought we would not be interested.
The family had no written or oral record of these songs but Tom was able to recall this one complete song and sang it for me. He and Maureen also were able to recall the occasions that gave rise to his compositions.

A local man Joe McBride got a new cooker, known as a Homepride, and it was a great attraction since most were cooking on open fires or ranges. The local women flocked to his house to try it out! Tommy saw the opportunity for a song in praise of the cooker.
Another song stimulus occurred with the acquisition by a local man called Cairns, of a particularly productive boar. The neighbours wheeled sows round in wheelbarrows to seek the attention of the boar. Tom recalled that in Tommy's song a sow had climbed into a wheelbarrow of its own accord, so eager was it for the encounter.
In another song of Tommy's, Maureen had the opening verse:

'I am a master tinker I'm famed both far and wide
I'm far above the tinker trade and I live on a laneside
The pots and pans and chambers and buckets are well made
But the only snag about this job I only get half paid.'

Tommy felt that the well-known ballad 'The Boys from the County Armagh' was too short and its ending was unsatisfactory, so he wrote an extra verse, sung for me by his daughter Dympna:

'And now that my rambling is over back home I'll return once more
To the sweetest wee spot under heaven its green hills and vales I adore
No more will I roam from my homeland no fortune will lure me afar
To lay me to rest with my kindred in my own native county Armagh.'

Tommy the Actor

Tommy was involved in local drama productions. According to *The Replay- A Parish History*:

'When one speaks of the past the names of the late Johnny Maguire, Stranooden; Tommy McCabe of Nart; Owen Mc Phillips of Nart and Frank Finlay are best remembered.'
Son Michael recalled when his father was asked to play a part in 'Professor Tim' he asked 'What part do you want me to play?' Because he knew them all.
He also featured in another George Shiels play 'Paul Twyning'.

Tommy the Bandsman

Tommy McCabe was involved with Hibernian bands. He played the flute and taught the bands flute music. He travelled to bands in Co. Armagh - Benburb, The Moy and Blackwatertown. These visits were also rewarding for picking up new songs.
There was a fife and drum band in Corcaghan which Mr. Barbour from Monaghan town came out to tutor, as Tommy recalls. Tommy also taught the Orange band from Loyst, a neighbouring townland, and he borrowed drums from them for the Hibernian bands. Relations were cordial between these organisations locally. Tommy visited the Nesbitt brothers who lived a few fields away to tutor them in music and the art of marching in time. He reported back that they made a decent job of playing the tunes but they just could not get the hang of marching in time!
He also remembered Archie Williamson, a local Orangeman, borrowing a Hibernian flute to play on the 12th of July. Archie was a little concerned that it might not play the right tunes!

A Good Neighbour

Tommy was always ready to lend a hand to anyone who needed it. Of course he lived at a time when, instead of paying for a job to be done, the philosophy of 'one good turn deserves another' was often the modus operandi. For example a carpentry job carried out by Stephen Mc Phillips or Tommy could be repaid by a day cutting turf in the bog. But Tommy went beyond reciprocal

arrangements. He used to cycle to Dundalk some Sundays (a distance of thirty miles) with Johnny Mc Phillips.
They passed the cemetery at Dartrey where the gravestones were covered in moss so the following Sunday he returned with a hammer and fine chisel to tidy them up.
Tommy was also a member of a mummer's group which collected for the needy around Christmas time.

Maureen's Memories of her Mother

Tommy's wife Bridget loved music and was a great lilter. She did not regard herself as a singer, but had a few party pieces.
Maureen remembers her mother getting second hand clothes from Belfast which she altered, ripping them and turning them inside out. She recalled one Sunday seeing about a dozen children wearing clothes she recognized as having been made by her mother. 'Wee peaked caps with pom- poms were part of the outfit.'
She also remembers a bag of dressing gowns, brought back from Aughnacloy, being turned into overcoats.
Bridget also worked from home for a shirt factory in Rockcorry. Her son Michael collected the tacked shirts from the factory for his mother to sew, and then brought them back to the factory when they were ready.
When she died after several bouts of illness, a lot of responsibilities fell on the shoulders of Tommy and the children.
'We did the milking in the morning before school and took the milk down the road on our way to the schoolhouse which was at the bottom of our lane. It was a Church of Ireland school but that was never an issue. In summer we went barefoot. After school the girls fed the calves and collected sticks. Often after tea the people would gather in the house for the music.'

Hiring

Tommy recounted how hiring was common in the county in the early to mid 1900's. Normally you hired for a six month period with a farmer. Journeyman workers went from area to area in search of work.

Owen McPhillips, a friend of Tommy, told how he was returning home from a card game on a dark evening when he heard a footstep on the road behind him – one that he did not recognize. The chap came up alongside and asked for a bed for the night. Owen offered him a bed and a few days' work as well. His name was Kevin Winters from Newry and he stayed around Monaghan working here and there for about a year. In fact he met and married a girl from Clontibret. He was a regular attender at the music gatherings and could contribute a song.

Tommy himself employed serving boys before he was married.

Johnny Maguire

Johnny from nearby Stranooden was a great friend of Tommy and collaborated with him in singing, writing and acting. He was a shopkeeper and a cattle dealer. Tommy remembers his shop being a great meeting place where the local news would be exchanged.

He and Tommy would go to local football or camogie matches, not so much to see the game, but rather to write verses about the antics of the managers and supporters on the sidelines.

Johnny had a keen sense of humour and would always help a neighbour out. A story is told about the local postman who had a habit of stretching out his walk longer than was necessary by visiting the pub before returning to the depot. Maguire got information that they were going to send out a young guy to monitor the postman on the following Tuesday. So he proceeded to send bogus letters to several people in the area – especially ones with long laneways!

He tipped the postman off and when his young observer turned up he told him he would have to run the route to get all the letters delivered in time.

So when the young man reported back he recommended that the time allocated for the postman's walk should be extended-not shortened!

Another example of Johnny's mischievous sense of humour occurred when he asked Frank Finlay to construct a new chimney for him. Finlay finished the job and told Maguire not to light a fire till the cement had dried. Johnny announced that he would invite the neighbours round for the first fire with the new chimney on the following Saturday. With the spectators assembled Johnny duly lit the fire.

But to Frank Finlay's horror the smoke billowed back down the chimney and engulfed the room. He climbed up to investigate and discovered that Johnny had covered the top of the chimney with a tile!

A friend of his had been in America for a long time and when he returned he found a lot had changed. Johnny Maguire expressed his feelings in the following lines:

32 Is this Corcaghan at all?

I have just returned to Ireland's isle from the land of Uncle Sam
For forty years I've toiled out there in a free and foreign land
But the people and the landmarks dear that I came back to see
Are not around Corcaghan which is very strange to me

Can anybody tell me where the good old folk have gone
The folk so gay that used to pray on a Sunday at Corcaghan
In October and May you'd find them when their hard day's work is done
Can anybody tell me where these good old folk have gone?

Where is old jolly Cassie that lived just at the cross?
Her house is down, the walls are there all overgrown with moss
In days gone by it took the eye it was so neat and clean
Now Cassie and her white-washed walls are nowhere to be seen

Where is saintly Father Murphy and his servant Miss McKeown?
Where's the white horse and the jaunting car and his jarvey Paddy Moen?
Where is Paddy Curley and his wife called Mary Ann?
They rang the bell in my young days in the chapel at Corcaghan

Where is Corney Leonard U. D.C. that owned the little pub?
Where is his wife that ran the pub with many a snap and snub?
Where's William Kieran that landed there each day with cleek and mell?*
'I've killed six pigs this morning,' is the story he would tell

Where is Owen Deighan who used to cart the butter from Cootehill?
For Eddie Graham to ship away the Englishmen to fill
Where's smithy Clarke that knocked the spark from the anvil thro' the door?
Where's Biddy Reilly, her paisley shawl, do you ever see her more?

Hadey's drawers I have not seen yet nor Windsors from the Roe
Thomas John and Tidy John or Clarke from Garranroe
Pat Mickey, Pat Quinn or Frank's Pat, the sir the soil the knob
I am sorry to say old Boylan gay is no longer in his job

The schoolhouse where I learned to write and often got the twig
Is now a house of animals, the horse, the cow, the pig
The master's gone his wife has gone, two I've missed most of all
Can anybody tell me is this Corcaghan at all?

*Implements used in the slaughter of pigs

I have just recently come across an old recording of Kathleen Duffy singing it. The tune is included with the others on the website.

Paddy the Poet

At the All-Ireland Fleadh in Clones (June 1968) Tommy introduced me to Paddy Brannigan, a poet who specialized in writing about topical issues. I recorded him reciting this poem about the outbreak of Foot and Mouth disease amongst farm animals in the UK in 1967, an event which led to widespread precautionary measures being taken in Ireland.

Now Irish lads and lasses in England far away
If you have intention to spend a holiday
It doesn't matter where you land officials you will meet
And I hope you will be kind enough to stop and dip your feet

If you come from an infected area as officials may suppose
They'll stand you up like ladders and disinfect your clothes
And then they'll send you to your home be it north or south
We're doin' our best endeavour to keep out the foot and mouth

You'll be confined unto your home for three weeks or maybe more
You'll be feelin' awful lonely and your heart it will be sore
You'll have no friends around you and no-one you can meet
And then you will be sorry that you didn't dip your feet

And when the time it comes along to go and cross the main
Swearing oaths and curses that you'll never come again
We may feel sorry for you but no matter how you pout
We're doin' our best endeavor to keep out the foot and mouth

Well the government up in Dublin they're doin' a job so fine
At last they have consented to send men to the border line
They are there I understand all strangers for to meet
But can they convince the smuggler to step to dip his feet?

The farmer has the law behind to preserve his land from sport
Trespassers will be summonsed and taken up to court
And then they'll pay a penalty and that's without a doubt
For we're doin' our best endeavour to keep out the foot and mouth

At churches on a Sunday I'm goin' to explain
Although you may be hurryin' admission for to gain
But let your conscience play its part and always be discreet
And never enter there unless you step and dip your feet

Now to conclude and finish one thing I have to say
The huntsmen they're not hunting no football do we play
And all ye lads and lasses that likes a dancing bout
Never dance with strangers they could have the foot and mouth

To Conclude

The McCabe family meeting with Fergus Woods and Marty Cullen [BBC] in March 2016 to record a feature for Radio Ulster's "New Voices".

My initial motivation was to publish the songs Gillian McPherson and I had collected from Tommy McCabe and the others all those years ago. As I talked with the McCabe family I began to realise that the story of Tommy was a lot more than the songs. I only got to share his friendship for a short period of time but when added to the memories I gathered from his children, I hope I have been able to give some insights into the man himself, his interests, his talents, his family and friends like Frank Finlay and Johnny Maguire, who themselves would have had wonderful stories to tell.

The account of the lives and songs of these people I have been able to give is but a snapshot of those times in a part of County Monaghan and by extension similar rural communities all over Ireland. It was clear to me even when I was talking to the singers that the way of life had passed which provided the context within which the songs were regularly sung. Speaking to members of the McCabe family over the years I have gained valuable insights into the world their father and his friends inhabited. The singers themselves are no longer alive and oral or written records are scarce.

But I am grateful that I had the opportunity to record these singers' songs and some of their stories. I hope this modest publication will help to ensure that their memories and the songs will be kept alive in their local area and beyond.

Sources

Alexander Turnbull Library, Wellington, New Zealand. Rare book department. Accession no. 110210 "Broadside Ballads Vol.2". Scrapbook of 305 broadsides. *The blooming maid of Rockcorry town.* By John Morris of Rockcorry. Belfast: Moore, Printer, 40 Ann Street {between 1852 and 1868}.

Broadside Ballad entitled 'The *Sorrowful Lamentation of Jane Sneddon for the loss of her lover, John Murray, at the late disaster at High Blantyre.'*
digital.nls.uk/broadsides/broadside.cfm/id/14972

Broadside Ballads Online. ballads.bodleian.ox.ac.uk

Buffalo NY Courier Feb 10 1896 Fulton History – *New York State Historical Newspapers. Captive Songsters* **fultonhistory.com** 0376 pdf

Child Ballad website. *The Gypsy Laddie (no 200)*
www.contemplator.com/child index.html

McConnell, Cathal, *I Have Travelled This Country.* Complied by Gerry O'Connor, Lughnasa Music 2011

Mc Mahon, Theo. *'More on Hugh Jackson and Crazy Jane'Clogher Record*, Vol xiii No2. 1989, pp 106-108. Accessed at Belfast Central Library

Michael Davitt Museum. Life of Michael Davitt, Straide, Foxford, County Mayo, Ireland. **www.museumsofmayo.com/davitt.html**

Morton, Robin. *Folksongs Sung in Ulster.* The Mercier Press 1970

Moulden, John. *Songs of Hugh McWilliams, schoolmaster 1831* Ulstersongs. Portrush. 1993

Moulden, John. *Thousands are Sailing: a brief song history of Irish emigration.* Ulstersongs. Portrush. 1994

Mulligan, Eamon and McCluskey, Fr.Brian. *The Replay. A Parish History* p198. Published by Sean McDermotts GFC. 1984

Murnane, James H and Peadar. *At the Ford of the Birches. The History of Ballybay, its people and vicinity* p282, p287. Published by Murnane Brothers. Sept 1999

Murray, Eamonn. The Mountain Lark column in *Northern Standard* 1933-1942. Accessed on microfilm at Clones Library, Co Monaghan

O'Lochlainn, Colm. *Irish Street Ballads* The Three Candles. Dublin, Ireland. 1939

O'Mordha, P.B *'Jackson and Jane' Clogher Record*, Vol iv No 3 1962 pp 197-200. Accessed at Belfast Central Library

Rooney, Mackie. *Monaghan Songs of Yesteryear*. Published by Comhaltas Ceoltóirí Éireann. 2011

Roud, Steve. *Folksong index and Broadside*. Vaughan Williams Memorial Library. **www.vwml.org**

Roud, Steve and Bishop, Julia. *The New Book of English Folk Songs*. P377. London. Penguin Classics. 2014

The Yorkshire Garland Group. **www.yorkshirefolksong.net/song_database/armatory/*The*_Bonny_Hawthorn.2aspx**

Washington Times. June 10 1913 *The Maid from Kinsale* **chroniclingamericaloc.gov/Iccn/sn84026749/1913-07-10/ed-1/seq-6pdf**

Recordings of versions of some of the songs

(In the order songs appear in the book)

The Banks of the Callan. Sarah Makem *As I roved out.* Musicals Tradition records. 2011

The Lass Among the Heather. Gillie Mc Pherson. *Common Ground.* Coop Breizll. 2002

Edward Boyle. Cathal McConnell. *Long Expectant Comes At Last.* Compass Records. 2000

Johnny, Lovely Johnny. Dolores Keane and John Faulkner. *Broken Hearted I'll Wander*. Mulligan Records. 2008

The High Walls of Derry. Vincent Doherty. *The High Walls of Derry*. 2013

The Maid of Kensale (Kinsale) Columbia Records. Published YouTube May2 2012

My Sweetheart in the Old Country. Gillie McPherson. *Common Ground.* Coop Breizll. 2002

Plains of Waterloo. Shirley and Dolly Collins. *Love,Death and the Lady*. Harvest. 1970
Martin Carthy. *The January Man.* Live in the Sunflower Folk Club, Belfast. 1978

Bonny Bunch of Roses. A.L. Lloyd. *English Street Songs*. Riverside. 1956
Seamus Ennis. *The Bonny Bunch of Roses*. Ember Records
Sam Larner. *A Garland for Sam*. BBC Records. 1974
Fred Jordan. *A Shropshire Lad*. Veteran. CD2 2003

When the Roses Bloom Again. Carter Family featuring Johnny Cash. *Keep on the Sunny Side*. Universe. 2013(re-issue)

Jackson and Jane. Five Hand Reel. *Earl of Moray*. RCA Victor. 1978
Gillie McPherson. *Common Ground*. Coop Breizll. 2002

Bunclody. Luke Kelly. *Luke Kelly the Collection*. CD 1994. i tunes IML 2008

The Gypsy Laddies. Jeannie Robertson. *Songs of a Scots Tinker Lady*. Quality Classics. 2011

57746738R00083

Made in the USA
Charleston, SC
24 June 2016